WORLD OF PLANTS

STEMS

BLACKBIRCH PRESS

An imprint of Thomson Gale, a part of The Th

THOMSON
GALE

Detroit • New York • San Francisco • San Diego • New Haven, Conn. • Waterville, Maine • London • Munich

THOMSON

GALE

Consultant: Kimi Hosoume
Associate Director of GEMS (Great
Explorations in Math and Science),
Director of PEACHES (Primary
Explorations for Adults, Children,
and Educators in Science),
Lawrence Hall of Science,
University of California,
Berkeley, California

For The Brown Reference Group plc
Editors: John Farndon and Angela Koo
Picture Researcher: Clare Newman
Design Manager: Lynne Ross
Managing Editor: Bridget Giles
Children's Publisher: Anne O'Daly
Production Director: Alastair Gourlay
Editorial Director: Lindsey Lowe

PHOTOGRAPHIC CREDITS

The Brown Reference Group plc: 5; **Corbis:** Larry Lee Photography 12,
Michele Westmorland 13; **PhotoDisc:** D. Falconer/PhotoLink 6;
Photos.com: 1, 3t, 4, 8, 9, 14/15, 15tr, 16c, 18, 19, 20, 21, 22.

Front Cover: Corbis: Thom Lang

LIBRARY OF CONGRESS CATALOGING-IN-PUBLICATION DATA

Farndon, John.
  Stems / by John Farndon.
    p. cm. — (World of plants)
  Includes bibliographical references and index.
  ISBN 1-4103-0420-5 (lib. : alk. paper)
  1. Roots (Botany)—Juvenile literature. I. Title

  QK646.F37 2005
  575.4—dc22

                                                    2005047049

Printed and bound in Thailand
10 9 8 7 6 5 4 3 2 1

Contents

Stems and plants   4

All about stems   6

Stems and animals   12

Stems and people   18

Glossary   23

Find out more   23

Index   24

Stems and plants

The stem or stalk is the tall, thin stick of a plant. It holds up all the leaves and the flowers.

As a plant grows, its stem usually gets taller and taller. As the stem grows upward, it provides a support for more and more leaves and flowers.

A plant's stem is not just a solid stick for the leaves and flowers to hang on. It is also a plant's main path. Inside every stem are lots of tiny pipes. The pipes carry water, food, and nutrients up and down between the plant's leaves and roots.

There are two kinds of pipes. Thin pipes carry water and chemicals up from the roots. These pipes are called xylem ("ZY-lum"). Thicker pipes carry food made in the leaves down to the rest of the plant. These pipes are called phloem ("FLO-em").

◀ Tulip stems
Tulip leaves grow from the base of the plant. Each thick green stem holds a single large flower.

Try This!

You can see how pipes in a stem carry water up to each flower with this experiment. Ask a grown-up to cut a white flower stem lengthways to about half way up. Wrap tape around the end of the cut. Then put each half stem in a different glass of water. Add drops of food color to one glass. Place by a sunny window. Look for traces of food color in the flowers with stems in colored water.

tape

split stem

water with food color

5

All about stems

Stems grow up from the ground. They start as little green spikes called shoots. Then they grow longer and longer.

▼ Giant redwood

The world's biggest stems belong to giant redwood trees. The tallest is 367 feet (112 meters) high. One is so wide, a car can drive through a hole in its trunk.

Some stems grow less than an inch tall. They get no thicker than a thread of cotton. But tree trunks can grow hundreds of feet tall. Trees are the tallest of all living things. They can sometimes also grow as thick as a house.

How a stem grows

A stem gets longer by growing at the tip. The tip is called a bud. The bud at the top of the stem is called the terminal bud. Buds can also grow on the side of the stem. These are called lateral, or secondary, buds. Lateral buds can become new shoots. These new shoots grow into lateral stems. Lateral buds can also grow into leaves or flowers.

✦ It's Amazing! ✦

Some plants have lots of stems. New stems called suckers grow up from the roots. Roots can spread far and wide underground. In Utah's Wasatch mountains, 47,000 stems of aspen trees have grown like this. Together they make the world's heaviest living thing, weighing more than 6,500 tons (6 million kilograms).

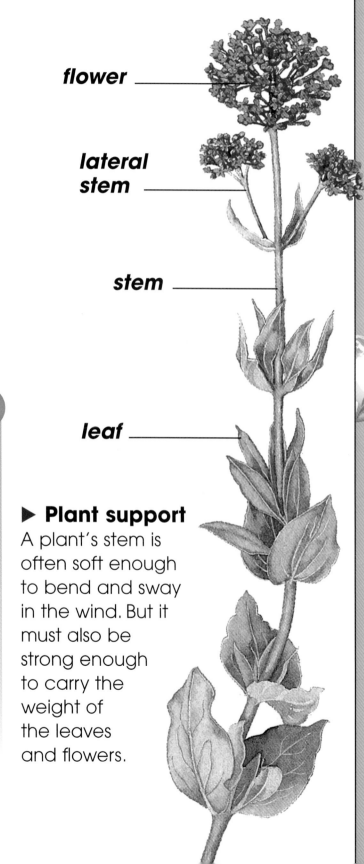

flower

lateral stem

stem

leaf

7

▶ Plant support

A plant's stem is often soft enough to bend and sway in the wind. But it must also be strong enough to carry the weight of the leaves and flowers.

Kinds of stems

▼ Climbing ivy
Ivy stems grow by climbing up a wall. Each stem puts out tiny roots with suckers that help it cling to the wall.

Some stems, like tree trunks, are simple upright sticks. But many plants have groups of two or more stems growing straight from the roots. Grass and many bushes have stems like this.

Clumps of stems help protect the plant from cold wind and hot sun. But clumps are often shorter than single stems. Plants that grow their stems in clumps are often shaded by other plants. That is why plants with clumped stems usually grow better in sunnier places, like open fields.

Climbing and ground stems

Many plants have thin winding stems that climb up walls, over fences, and along tree trunks and branches. Beans, grapevines, ivy, honeysuckle, and morning glory are all climbers. Climbing helps the plant spread and reach toward the sun without growing a thick trunk like a tree. The plant grows little hooks and suckers that help it hold on.

Some stems, like sweet potatoes and cucumbers, grow along the ground.

It's Amazing!

The world's fastest growing stems belong to some kinds of bamboos. Bamboo grows in Asia. It belongs to the grass family but has slender wooden stems. Some bamboos can grow 3 feet (1 meter) a day and reach more than 100 feet (30 meters) high in three months!

Underground stems

Some plants are able to make the most of the weather. In summer, their leaves make lots of food. But the plants do not use all the food. Instead, they store some food in a thick stem underground. The stem lies safe in the soil through the winter. In spring, the food in the stem helps the plant grow again.

There are four kinds of underground stems. They are called bulbs, rhizomes, corms, and tubers. A bulb is a stubby underground stem with layers like an onion. A rhizome is a stem that grows sideways underground. A corm is like a bulb but without layers. A tuber is a knobby lump.

▶ **An iris flower**
has a sausage-shaped rhizome. New shoots and roots grow from it. Mints and many grasses have rhizomes, too.

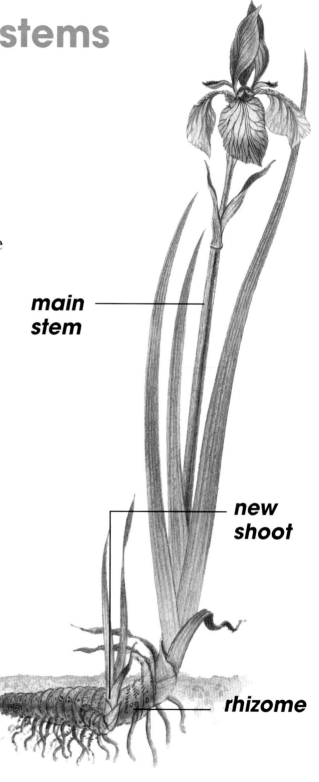

main stem

new shoot

rhizome

▼ Onion bulb

There are many layers inside an onion. These layers are called scales. Each scale is a leaf swollen with stored food. Right at the center of the onion is a new plant waiting to grow.

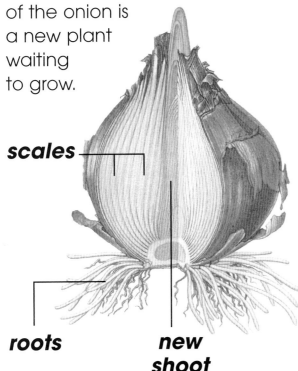

scales

roots

new shoot

★ *It's Amazing!* ★

The most familiar tubers are potatoes. The world's biggest tuber, however, belongs to the Titan arum of Sumatra in Southeast Asia. The giant tuber is as big and heavy as an oil drum. It can weigh more than 170 pounds (77 kilograms). It flowers only twice in 40 years. But when the flowers do grow, they are the biggest in the world.

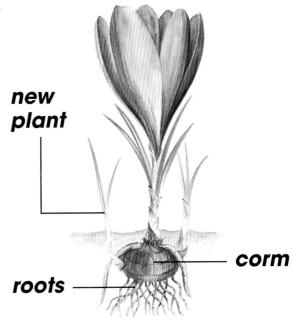

new plant

corm

roots

▶ Crocus corm

A crocus plant has a typical corm. A corm grows upright, not sideways like a rhizome. It is fleshy and looks like a bulb. New plants grow from the corm.

11

Stems and animals

Many animals depend on plant stems to stay alive. Some animals use stems to make homes. Some eat stems.

Many animals build nests to make a safe, warm home. Sticks, twigs, grass, and other plant stems are good for building nests. Chimpanzees, orangutans, and gorillas build nests of twigs. They make their nests in the trees to sleep in at night. Most rodents such as mice and squirrels built nests, too. But the best nest builders are birds.

Sticks for nests

Birds use stems to make nests to lay their eggs in and keep their chicks safe. Stems can be built into all kinds of different nests. Big, thin sticks can be laid together to make a flat nest. Flat nests are called platform nests.

It's Amazing!

Beavers use sticks to build a dam across a stream (left). The biggest beaver dams are up to 1,000 feet (330 meters) long. The dam creates a pond of deep water. The beaver can then build a nest out in the middle of the pond. This keeps them safe from dangerous animals.

Storks and eagles build platform nests in tree tops and on cliffs. Short sticks and twigs can be twisted together to make neat, cup-shaped nests in trees. Small birds like thrushes make nests like these. Goldcrests make fancy nests that hang like balls. The most amazing hanging nests are made by weaver birds.

▲ Weaver town

Weaver birds use sticks to build one giant nest together. Their nest is home to hundreds of birds. The dark holes in the nest are doorways for the birds.

13

Stems for food

Many kinds of animals use plant stems for food. Older, woody stems are often too tough to eat. They do not have many nutrients in them either. But young and tender shoots make good food. Animals that eat shoots and leaves are called browsers. Most browsers, such as deer and moose, live in woodlands.

The biggest browsers

There is lots of food to eat on a tree if an animal can reach it. So some browsing animals grow very big, especially in Africa. Some of the world's biggest and tallest animals live in Africa. They are all browsers. Biggest of all are elephants. Elephants use their trunks to reach the softest shoots at the tops of trees.

Giraffes are even taller. They can use their long necks to reach twigs and leaves 20 feet (6 meters) up in the air. Giraffes eat trees with sharp thorns. But a giraffe's leathery mouth lets it eat the thorny stems without getting hurt.

▼ Summer food

In the winter, many deer eat twigs to survive. In spring and summer, however, they can eat the tasty new shoots and leaves.

It's Amazing!

Woodpeckers feed on insects that live inside tree trunks. To get the insects, a woodpecker holds onto the tree and hammers away with its beak. Eventually it makes it right through to the insects' tunnels. The bird sticks its tongue in and licks out a tasty meal. The woodpecker's tongue is very long—longer than the bird itself. The tongue has a sticky tip for catching insects.

Spines, thorns, and stings

Plants cannot run away or hide like animals when they are attacked. But they can keep themselves safe in other ways. Some plants are poisonous to eat, like oleanders. Other plants have leaves that give a sharp sting, like nettles.

In dry places, juicy plant stems look good to hungry and thirsty animals. So many plants that live in dry places have long spines and thorns that keep the animals away. Acacia thorn trees have long spines. The honey locust tree has the sharpest spines.

thorns

▶ **Rose thorns**
Roses are pretty flowers. But their stems can have very sharp thorns. Few animals can eat a stem with thorns like these.

The honey locust tree's spines can be up to 6 inches (15 centimeters) long and have three spikes at the end.

Each spine is a needlelike leaf.

It's Amazing!

Thorns of Mexican acacia trees work in an unusual way. Normally, thorns keep animals away. But ants live inside the thorns. The ants scare away other insects. Once a year the tree flowers. It needs bees to come and take pollen from its flowers. The flowers smell bad to the ants, so they stay away and do not frighten off the bees. When the flowers die, the ants come back.

stem

17

◀ Cactus plant

Cactuses grow in dry places like deserts. They have fat, juicy green stems. The stem has prickly spines to stop animals from eating it.

Stems and people

People eat plant stems. People also use stems as wood to build homes or as firewood for cooking and heating.

Most plant stems are too tough and stringy to eat. But some are soft and juicy enough to eat when they are young. Asparagus is a plant stem. Bamboo gets very tough when it is old, but tiny new shoots are soft and tasty. Bamboo shoots are used a lot in Chinese cooking. Sometimes the best part of a stem for eating grows underground. Onions, potatoes, and ginger are all underground stems.

Some stems give us material for clothing. Stems of flax are broken into fibers to make into linen cloth. Different bits of a stem can provide different things. The bark around the trunk of cork oak trees makes cork. Willow tree bark provides aspirin. Rubber, eucalyptus oil, and tea-tree oil all come from the sticky juices that flow in tree trunks.

▼ Celery stems

These might look like stems. In fact, the part we eat is the stalk of the leaves. Celery's stem is very short and right in the middle of the plant.

◄ Sugar cane

is a kind of grass with tough, woody stems. The sweet juice inside the stems is used to make sugar. To get the sugar, the stems must be chopped up, then boiled in water to make a sweet syrup.

It's Amazing!

Maple syrup is the sap of the maple tree. An Iroquois legend tells how it was discovered. One day a chief named Woksis threw his tomahawk at a tree. When he pulled it out, the tree's sap dripped into his wife's water bowl. She used it for cooking—and liked it!

Building with stems

People have used plant stems to make tools and shelters since very early times. Early people used thick stems for ax handles. They used soft, bendable stems to make bows.

The first shelters and houses were made from woody plant stems. The remains of the world's oldest house are in Japan. The house was built from sticks 600,000 years ago.

◄ Log cabin
In places where forests grow, wood is the perfect building material. This house amongst the trees is made all of wood.

★ It's Amazing! ★

Most wood is marked with dark lines called grain. These lines show where the tree stopped growing at the end of each summer. Wood's strength and springiness depend on the grain. Wooden baseball bats are usually made from the wood of ash or maple trees. But batmakers must take care to select only wood with a straight grain. They then shape the wood so the grain lies along the length of the bat.

Wood and timber

Wood is the material that makes up the trunk or stem of a tree. When wood is used for crafts or building, it is called timber. Wood is very strong, but it can be cut and carved easily. Timber is cut into logs, and logs are cut into planks.

More than a billion trees are cut down every year around the world to make wood. New trees are grown to replace many of those that are cut down. Not all wood is used for timber. A lot of wood is crushed and turned into mushy pulp. Pulp is used to make paper.

Burning wood

Prehistoric people discovered how to set alight sticks to make fires 1.5 million years ago. With a fire they could keep themselves warm in winter. They could also cook tough meat to make it easier to eat.

A hundred years ago, 90 percent of Americans burned wood to heat their homes. In poorer countries, more than 80 percent of all people still burn sticks to keep warm and do all their cooking.

◀ Log fire

When wood burns, it makes flames and glows bright red. Gases in the wood burn, making the flames. The wood glows because it gets very hot. Wood must be very dry to burn well. Damp wood will smoke. It may not even burn at all.

Glossary

browser an animal that feeds on shoots and leaves.

bud a tip on a stem that grows into a new shoot or flower.

bulb a thick undergound stem made from layers called scales.

corm a thick underground stem like a bulb but without layers.

lateral bud a bud that grows on the side of a stem.

phloem the thick pipes that carry food down through a stem.

rhizome a stem that grows sideways underground.

sap the sticky juice inside a plant stem.

scales the layers in a bulb.

secondary bud another name for a lateral bud.

shoot a new young stem.

terminal bud the bud at the tip or end of a stem.

tuber an underground stem that forms a knobbly lump.

xylem the thin pipes that carry water and chemicals up through a plant stem.

23

★ Find out more ★

Books
Laura Howell, Kirsteen Rogers, and Corinne Henderson. **World of Plants.** EDC Publishing, New York, 2002.
Sally Morgan. **Roots, Stems and Leaves.** Chrysalis, NY, 2004.

Web sites
Ecotree: Inside a stem
www.botany.uwc.ac.za/ ecotree/trunkb.htm

Index

acacia trees 16-17
ants 17
asparagus 18
aspirin 19

bamboo 9, 18
baseball bats 21
beavers 12
browsers 14
bud 7

cactus 17
celery 19
climbers 9
clothing 19

deer 14–15

fire 22

ginger 18
giraffes 14
grain 21
grass 8–9, 10

houses 20

iris 10
ivy 8–9

maple syrup 19

nests 12–13

oleanders 16
onion 10–11, 18

paper 21

redwood tree 6
rhizome 10
roses 16
rubber 19

shoots 6–7, 14–15, 16–17
suckers 7, 8–9
sugar cane 19

thorns 16–17
tuber 10–11

weaver birds 13
willow 19
wood 20–21, 22
woodpeckers 15